You are more powerful than you know.

JOURNAL FOR:

_____

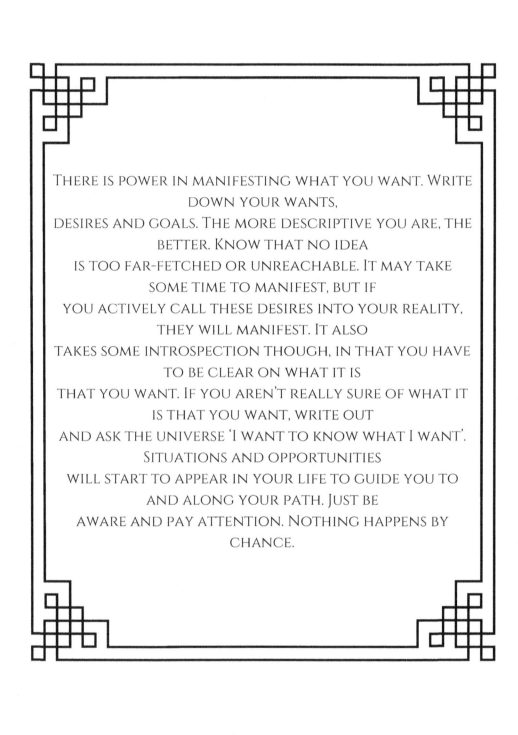

There is power in manifesting what you want. Write down your wants,
desires and goals. The more descriptive you are, the better. Know that no idea
is too far-fetched or unreachable. It may take some time to manifest, but if
you actively call these desires into your reality, they will manifest. It also
takes some introspection though, in that you have to be clear on what it is
that you want. If you aren't really sure of what it is that you want, write out
and ask the universe 'I want to know what I want'. Situations and opportunities
will start to appear in your life to guide you to and along your path. Just be
aware and pay attention. Nothing happens by chance.

Date:

What do you desire?

WRITE DOWN ONE WAY TO ACTIVELY WORK TOWARDS THESE DESIRES.

Date:

What do you desire?

WRITE DOWN ONE WAY TO ACTIVELY WORK TOWARDS THESE DESIRES.

Date:

What do you desire?

Date:

What do you desire?

WRITE DOWN ONE WAY TO ACTIVELY WORK TOWARDS THESE DESIRES.

Date:

What do you desire?

WRITE DOWN ONE WAY TO ACTIVELY WORK TOWARDS THESE DESIRES.

Date:

What do you desire?

WRITE DOWN ONE WAY TO ACTIVELY WORK TOWARDS THESE DESIRES.

Date:

What do you desire?

WRITE DOWN ONE WAY TO ACTIVELY WORK TOWARDS THESE DESIRES.

Date:

What do you desire?

WRITE DOWN ONE WAY TO ACTIVELY WORK TOWARDS THESE DESIRES.

Date:

What do you desire?

WRITE DOWN ONE WAY TO ACTIVELY WORK TOWARDS THESE DESIRES.

Date:

What do you desire?

WRITE DOWN ONE WAY TO ACTIVELY WORK TOWARDS THESE DESIRES.

Date:

What do you desire?

WRITE DOWN ONE WAY TO ACTIVELY WORK TOWARDS THESE DESIRES.

Date:

What do you desire?

WRITE DOWN ONE WAY TO ACTIVELY WORK TOWARDS THESE DESIRES.

Date:

What do you desire?

WRITE DOWN ONE WAY TO ACTIVELY WORK TOWARDS THESE DESIRES.

Date:

What do you desire?

WRITE DOWN ONE WAY TO ACTIVELY WORK TOWARDS THESE DESIRES.

Date:

What do you desire?

WRITE DOWN ONE WAY TO ACTIVELY WORK TOWARDS THESE DESIRES.

Date:

What do you desire?

WRITE DOWN ONE WAY TO ACTIVELY WORK TOWARDS THESE DESIRES.

Date:

What do you desire?

WRITE DOWN ONE WAY TO ACTIVELY WORK TOWARDS THESE DESIRES.

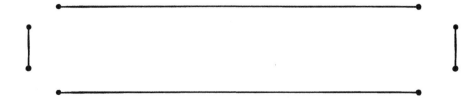

What do you desire?

WRITE DOWN ONE WAY TO ACTIVELY WORK TOWARDS THESE DESIRES.

Date:

What do you desire?

WRITE DOWN ONE WAY TO ACTIVELY WORK TOWARDS THESE DESIRES.

Date:

What do you desire?

WRITE DOWN ONE WAY TO ACTIVELY WORK TOWARDS THESE DESIRES.

Date:

What do you desire?

WRITE DOWN ONE WAY TO ACTIVELY WORK TOWARDS THESE DESIRES.

What do you desire?

WRITE DOWN ONE WAY TO ACTIVELY WORK TOWARDS THESE DESIRES.

Date:

What do you desire?

WRITE DOWN ONE WAY TO ACTIVELY WORK TOWARDS THESE DESIRES.

Date:

What do you desire?

WRITE DOWN ONE WAY TO ACTIVELY WORK TOWARDS THESE DESIRES.

Date:

What do you desire?

WRITE DOWN ONE WAY TO ACTIVELY WORK TOWARDS THESE DESIRES.

What do you desire?

WRITE DOWN ONE WAY TO ACTIVELY WORK TOWARDS THESE DESIRES.

Date:

What do you desire?

WRITE DOWN ONE WAY TO ACTIVELY WORK TOWARDS THESE DESIRES.

What do you desire?

WRITE DOWN ONE WAY TO ACTIVELY WORK TOWARDS THESE DESIRES.

Date:

What do you desire?

WRITE DOWN ONE WAY TO ACTIVELY WORK TOWARDS THESE DESIRES.

Date:

What do you desire?

WRITE DOWN ONE WAY TO ACTIVELY WORK TOWARDS THESE DESIRES.

Date:

| **What do you desire?** |

WRITE DOWN ONE WAY TO ACTIVELY WORK TOWARDS THESE DESIRES.

Date:

What do you desire?

_____

_____

_____

_____

_____

_____

_____

_____

_____

_____

_____

_____

_____

_____

_____

_____

_____

_____

WRITE DOWN ONE WAY TO ACTIVELY WORK TOWARDS THESE DESIRES.

Date:

What do you desire?

WRITE DOWN ONE WAY TO ACTIVELY WORK TOWARDS THESE DESIRES.

Date:

What do you desire?

WRITE DOWN ONE WAY TO ACTIVELY WORK TOWARDS THESE DESIRES.

What do you desire?

WRITE DOWN ONE WAY TO ACTIVELY WORK TOWARDS THESE DESIRES.

Date:

What do you desire?

WRITE DOWN ONE WAY TO ACTIVELY WORK TOWARDS THESE DESIRES.

Date:

What do you desire?

WRITE DOWN ONE WAY TO ACTIVELY WORK TOWARDS THESE DESIRES.

Date:

What do you desire?

WRITE DOWN ONE WAY TO ACTIVELY WORK TOWARDS THESE DESIRES.

Date:

What do you desire?

WRITE DOWN ONE WAY TO ACTIVELY WORK TOWARDS THESE DESIRES.

What do you desire?

WRITE DOWN ONE WAY TO ACTIVELY WORK TOWARDS THESE DESIRES.

Date:

What do you desire?

WRITE DOWN ONE WAY TO ACTIVELY WORK TOWARDS THESE DESIRES.

What do you desire?

WRITE DOWN ONE WAY TO ACTIVELY WORK TOWARDS THESE DESIRES.

Date:

What do you desire?

WRITE DOWN ONE WAY TO ACTIVELY WORK TOWARDS THESE DESIRES.

Date:

What do you desire?

WRITE DOWN ONE WAY TO ACTIVELY WORK TOWARDS THESE DESIRES.

Date:

What do you desire?

WRITE DOWN ONE WAY TO ACTIVELY WORK TOWARDS THESE DESIRES.

Date:

What do you desire?

WRITE DOWN ONE WAY TO ACTIVELY WORK TOWARDS THESE DESIRES.

Date:

What do you desire?

WRITE DOWN ONE WAY TO ACTIVELY WORK TOWARDS THESE DESIRES.

What do you desire?

WRITE DOWN ONE WAY TO ACTIVELY WORK TOWARDS THESE DESIRES.

Date:

What do you desire?

WRITE DOWN ONE WAY TO ACTIVELY WORK TOWARDS THESE DESIRES.

What do you desire?

WRITE DOWN ONE WAY TO ACTIVELY WORK TOWARDS THESE DESIRES.

Date:

What do you desire?

WRITE DOWN ONE WAY TO ACTIVELY WORK TOWARDS THESE DESIRES.

Date:

What do you desire?

WRITE DOWN ONE WAY TO ACTIVELY WORK TOWARDS THESE DESIRES.

Date:

What do you desire?

WRITE DOWN ONE WAY TO ACTIVELY WORK TOWARDS THESE DESIRES.

Date:

What do you desire?

WRITE DOWN ONE WAY TO ACTIVELY WORK TOWARDS THESE DESIRES.

What do you desire?

WRITE DOWN ONE WAY TO ACTIVELY WORK TOWARDS THESE DESIRES.

What do you desire?

WRITE DOWN ONE WAY TO ACTIVELY WORK TOWARDS THESE DESIRES.

What do you desire?

WRITE DOWN ONE WAY TO ACTIVELY WORK TOWARDS THESE DESIRES.

Date:

What do you desire?

WRITE DOWN ONE WAY TO ACTIVELY WORK TOWARDS THESE DESIRES.

Date:

What do you desire?

WRITE DOWN ONE WAY TO ACTIVELY WORK TOWARDS THESE DESIRES.

Date:

What do you desire?

WRITE DOWN ONE WAY TO ACTIVELY WORK TOWARDS THESE DESIRES.

Date:

What do you desire?

WRITE DOWN ONE WAY TO ACTIVELY WORK TOWARDS THESE DESIRES.

Date:

What do you desire?

WRITE DOWN ONE WAY TO ACTIVELY WORK TOWARDS THESE DESIRES.

Date:

What do you desire?

WRITE DOWN ONE WAY TO ACTIVELY WORK TOWARDS THESE DESIRES.

What do you desire?

WRITE DOWN ONE WAY TO ACTIVELY WORK TOWARDS THESE DESIRES.

Date:

What do you desire?

WRITE DOWN ONE WAY TO ACTIVELY WORK TOWARDS THESE DESIRES.

Date:

What do you desire?

WRITE DOWN ONE WAY TO ACTIVELY WORK TOWARDS THESE DESIRES.

What do you desire?

WRITE DOWN ONE WAY TO ACTIVELY WORK TOWARDS THESE DESIRES.

Date:

What do you desire?

WRITE DOWN ONE WAY TO ACTIVELY WORK TOWARDS THESE DESIRES.

What do you desire?

WRITE DOWN ONE WAY TO ACTIVELY WORK TOWARDS THESE DESIRES.

Date:

What do you desire?

WRITE DOWN ONE WAY TO ACTIVELY WORK TOWARDS THESE DESIRES.

Date:

What do you desire?

WRITE DOWN ONE WAY TO ACTIVELY WORK TOWARDS THESE DESIRES.

Date:

What do you desire?

WRITE DOWN ONE WAY TO ACTIVELY WORK TOWARDS THESE DESIRES.

Date:

What do you desire?

WRITE DOWN ONE WAY TO ACTIVELY WORK TOWARDS THESE DESIRES.

Date:

What do you desire?

WRITE DOWN ONE WAY TO ACTIVELY WORK TOWARDS THESE DESIRES.

Date:

What do you desire?

WRITE DOWN ONE WAY TO ACTIVELY WORK TOWARDS THESE DESIRES.

Date:

What do you desire?

WRITE DOWN ONE WAY TO ACTIVELY WORK TOWARDS THESE DESIRES.

Date:

What do you desire?

WRITE DOWN ONE WAY TO ACTIVELY WORK TOWARDS THESE DESIRES.

Date:

What do you desire?

WRITE DOWN ONE WAY TO ACTIVELY WORK TOWARDS THESE DESIRES.

Date:

What do you desire?

WRITE DOWN ONE WAY TO ACTIVELY WORK TOWARDS THESE DESIRES.

Date:

What do you desire?

WRITE DOWN ONE WAY TO ACTIVELY WORK TOWARDS THESE DESIRES.

Date:

What do you desire?

WRITE DOWN ONE WAY TO ACTIVELY WORK TOWARDS THESE DESIRES.

Date:

What do you desire?

WRITE DOWN ONE WAY TO ACTIVELY WORK TOWARDS THESE DESIRES.

Date:

What do you desire?

WRITE DOWN ONE WAY TO ACTIVELY WORK TOWARDS THESE DESIRES.

Date:

What do you desire?

WRITE DOWN ONE WAY TO ACTIVELY WORK TOWARDS THESE DESIRES.

Date:

What do you desire?

WRITE DOWN ONE WAY TO ACTIVELY WORK TOWARDS THESE DESIRES.

Date:

What do you desire?

WRITE DOWN ONE WAY TO ACTIVELY WORK TOWARDS THESE DESIRES.

Date:

What do you desire?

WRITE DOWN ONE WAY TO ACTIVELY WORK TOWARDS THESE DESIRES.

What do you desire?

WRITE DOWN ONE WAY TO ACTIVELY WORK TOWARDS THESE DESIRES.

Date:

What do you desire?

WRITE DOWN ONE WAY TO ACTIVELY WORK TOWARDS THESE DESIRES.

What do you desire?

WRITE DOWN ONE WAY TO ACTIVELY WORK TOWARDS THESE DESIRES.

Date:

What do you desire?

WRITE DOWN ONE WAY TO ACTIVELY WORK TOWARDS THESE DESIRES.

What do you desire?

Date:

What do you desire?

WRITE DOWN ONE WAY TO ACTIVELY WORK TOWARDS THESE DESIRES.

Date:

What do you desire?

WRITE DOWN ONE WAY TO ACTIVELY WORK TOWARDS THESE DESIRES.

Date:

What do you desire?

WRITE DOWN ONE WAY TO ACTIVELY WORK TOWARDS THESE DESIRES.

Date:

What do you desire?

WRITE DOWN ONE WAY TO ACTIVELY WORK TOWARDS THESE DESIRES.

Date:

What do you desire?

WRITE DOWN ONE WAY TO ACTIVELY WORK TOWARDS THESE DESIRES.

Date:

What do you desire?

WRITE DOWN ONE WAY TO ACTIVELY WORK TOWARDS THESE DESIRES.

Made in the USA
Middletown, DE
06 December 2022

16099536R00057